Mastering Multi-Band Compression

17 step by step multiband compression techniques for getting flawless mixes

Nathan Nyquist

Mastering Multi-Band Compression:

17 step by step multiband compression techniques for getting flawless mixes

Copyright © 2018 Nathan Nyquist. All rights reserved.

Protected by copyright laws of the United States and international treaties.

No part of this publication in whole or in part may be copied, duplicated, reproduced, or transmitted in any form or by any means, electronic or mechanical, including photocopying, recording, or by any information storage and retrieval system, without the express written permission from the publisher.

Copyright and other intellectual property laws protect these materials and any unauthorized reproduction or retransmission will constitute an infringement of copyright law.

Federal law provides severe civil and criminal penalties for the unauthorized reproduction, distribution, or exhibition of copyrighted materials. Penalties for criminal and statutory copyright infringement are set forth at 18 U.S.C § 2319.

ISBN: 9781982917128

Table of Contents

Introduction 1
What Most Engineers Won't Tell You About Compression 7
The 3 Truths About Compression 9
It's Not Multiband Compression, it's Dynamic EQing 13
Multiband Compression Controls Explained 19
4-Zone Mix Theory 29
Blend/Contrast Theory and Multiband Compression 33
    Transient Control for Blend/Contrast 36
    Volume Leveling for Blend/Contrast 37
Don't Aim for Perfection, Aim for Good Enough 41
Where to Use Multiband Compression 47
17 Powerful Multiband Compression Techniques 49
    (1 – 2) Transient Control Techniques 55
    Transient Enhancement of Plucky Sounds 55
    Transient Reduction of Plucky Sounds 59
    (3 - 4) Volume Leveling 63
    Controlling Sweeping Resonant Peaks 67
    Controlling Frequency Peaks at the Group/Bus Level 69
    (5 – 17) Collection of Techniques 73
    Shaping Snare Body 73
    Shaping Snare Snap 76
    Adding Kick Punch 77
    Removing Kick Woofiness 79
    Strengthening the Body of a Sound 82

Compressing Sub Frequencies for More Power 84

Multiband Compressing for Increased Front/Back Depth 87

Multiband Compressing Reverb for Increased Front/Back Depth ... 91

Sidechain Multiband Compression for Increased Kick Punch 94

Sidechain Multiband Compression for Improved Lead Clarity 97

Vocal De-Essing 99

Broadcast Vocals 102

Mastering Multiband Compression 107

Zen and the Art of Multiband Compression 117

Introduction

Multiband compression is one of the most nebulous and confusing tools in a mixers tool chest. It's no surprise because compression by itself is difficult for a lot of people to figure out.

In this book I'm going to be giving you the step by step techniques for using multiband compression. By using these techniques you'll avoid any confusion and discover the true power of multiband compression.

This isn't going to be another wishy-washy, difficult to grasp book on mixing theory. But at the same time I'm not going to grossly over-simplify things. We'll be going as deep as we need to and we'll only be taking what's necessary.

I'm a big fan of the painter Bob Ross. He was a soothingly voiced, afro-haired man who would paint watercolors on public television back in the 80s. Because it was so relaxing and enjoyable, people liked watching and falling asleep to him as he painted—it's very therapeutic.

Bob never believed in mistakes, only "Happy Accidents." And this is the one thing I hope you'll remember because it applies everywhere. Every accident is really just an opportunity to go in a new and exciting direction.

Often people will 'be incredible' without noticing, simply because they're used to it, but for somebody a little behind, one action can change everything.

It was after Bob's umpteenth explanation of how he got a result that I realized he literally just had a mental preset for everything he wanted. He knew the exact, repeatable steps he needed to get a result and he didn't torture himself by thinking he had to reinvent the wheel.

I remember after that realization thinking to myself, "Why don't I do the same thing for music?"

"Do what??" Said pretentious and unproductive inner Nathan.

"Just have preset ways of doing things so I never get stuck again and continually get the joy of great sounding and finished tracks."

Pretentious Nathan Scoffed. He'd been pretentiously not making any music for 2 years. The idea of using presets was alien to him and a violation of his artistic integrity.

I very much enjoyed pretentious Nathan's squirming at the thought of coming up with formulaic and preset ways of doing things. He couldn't make a song for shit and honestly needed to go die in a ditch somewhere about two years earlier. Unfortunately ego's can't die because they aren't real and the price of their death is my body. I'm pretty attached to my body.

Anyway I knew I was sick and tired of getting stuck, so it wasn't even difficult for me to go to work and begin finding ways to make a formula for everything I did.

I was already obsessed about Audio Engineering. Audio engineering naturally aligns with the part of me that likes nothing but looking for problems and solving them. It will finish problems and then go looking for more, and if there aren't any problems it will just invent them. Sound familiar?

That also happens to be the part of me that is about as capable of finishing a song as brick could discover the cure for cancer. Unfortunately for 2 years that truth wasn't clear enough to stop my inner brick from trying to make music.

Now rather than say writers block as if it's this curse, I'm going to say what was really happening because I was simply being uncreative at finding simple and novel ways to finish a song.

Luckily writer's block wasn't a complete waste, because in those two years all I did was audio engineering and sound design.

Because of that and the years since, I've gotten to a point where I've merged all my obsessive and perfectionist desires with the elegant and simple, preset approach to making music that Bob Ross first inspired in me.

As a result of this, the techniques in this book are incredibly simple and they will get you the sound you're after. They will also free up tons of mental energy which will enable you to spend more time exploring your mixes instead of desperately trying to shovel your way out of problem after problem. I don't want multiband compression to be a problem for you ever again.

If you know anything about my mixing philosophy then you know that I'm always aiming for 70% of my instruments to blend together and 30% of my instruments to contrast against that blended backdrop.

The 70/30 split allows me to achieve more vibrant levels of detail and separation in my mixes. Because of this rule a mix becomes increasingly more spacious and clear the more it's followed.

This is how we create depth. Depth is in fact the exacted result of the formulaic processes I teach.

In the end mixing is art and I want this art to feel second nature to you. I already went through my juvenile phase of hating on presets and it only slowed down my progress. Once I realized that presets aren't just tutorials, my skills improved geometrically.

I'm telling you this because at every level of mixing my primary goal is to simplify the process with set and forget presets.

I do this in reverence of Bob Ross but also because every skilled producer/engineer I've met does this to some degree. Whether we realize it or not, habitual mix decisions are in fact presets.

As my students have already discovered in **The 3-Space Reverb Framework** and **The Bus Compression Framework**, some of the most difficult parts of mixing are actually very formulaic. This means they can be replicated and repeated for consistent results across many mediums.

Given the topic of this book, I'm assuming you at least have a basic understanding of EQ and Compression. If not then I would suggest getting a copy of **The EQ and Compression Formula** as it covers my entire perspective on EQ and Compression and how they work together.

In the beginning sections of this book I'll be covering everything you need to know about multiband compression before even using it. I've then meticulously gone step by step through each of the 17 ways we use multiband compression. This means I'll explain exactly how each of the techniques works as well as how to tweak it for your needs.

So before we jump into multi-band compression I want to give you my personal definition of what a regular, single-band compressor is.

This is important because a multiband compressor is really just an EQ that has a regular (single-band) compressor attached to each EQ band.

This is why we are beginning our journey by explaining what a single-band compressor *actually is*. So let's get into it.

What Most Engineers Won't Tell You About Compression

Compression is just a way for us to control volume. **It is absolutely no different than your finger on a volume fader**. Where it gets tricky for most people is that they learn about compression and then continue to think of compression as just compression.

Unfortunately, compression is a pretty vague word. It can mean a lot of different things, and one thing meaning many things is bad for learning. In order for you to understand compression it can't mean many things. It can only mean one and I want compression for you to mean an **Automatic Volume Fader.**

Why are we redefining it as an automatic volume fader? I'll answer that with an example of a common exchange between a student and a teacher:

What exactly are you compressing said the student.

"Dynamics"

What are dynamics?

"It's the differences in volume"

What differences?

"Well there are loud parts and quieter parts, and we want to bring them closer together so there's less dynamic range," proudly said the teacher.

Why?

"Because it sounds good."

Why?

"..... Just don't use it if you don't know why you're using it."

This teacher/student conversation and its variations have been happening for decades. But it could have all been avoided if they started with something the student already understands—a volume fader.

Everyone knows what a volume fader is and if we begin to look at a compressor as just an **automatic volume fader**, then it becomes much easier to use. Don't worry about the automatic part, because we'll be explaining that in a little.

The 3 Truths About Compression

In the beginning, god created the earth, people, global warming and then music. After listening to music he quickly created the volume fader.

One of god's non-deterministic children became an audio engineer and through intense industry and research created the dynamic range 'compressor.'

The things we create when we're looking for answers to meaningful questions are beautiful. As an artist I want to show you how to create more beautiful music by using an **automatic volume fader**.

So let's begin with the 3 truths about compression also known as **automatic volume fading**.

Truth #1

A compressor is just an automatic volume fader.

You've already heard this, but lets go a little deeper into what I mean. A volume fader controls how loud or quiet something is. The way it becomes automatic is when you give it a way of increasing or decreasing the volume of something without the need for your finger on it.

What allows a compressor to function automatically are the controls which give you a way to set it and forget it so it does exactly what you want.

The parameters that allow for this automatic functioning in particular are **Threshold, Ratio, Attack and Release**. These are like the cruise control on a car that allows it to automatically adjust and stay at the right speed.

Truth #2

Anything a compressor can do, volume automation can do.

You probably already know how you can literally shape a sound by volume automating it. If you don't then you certainly know how you can make a long decay hi-hat sound like a closed hi-hat just by shortening the length of its volume tail. This is volume automation.

Since compression is just doing what your finger can do on a fader, but automatically, then it's the same thing as volume automation.

They're both fingerless activities in the end and that's good because for the most part we've only got 10 and we'll need all 10 fingers to turn our mixes up to 11.

Truth #3

Compressors make loud sounds quieter

I'm not the biggest fan of this definition, because I think it gets misrepresented so let me reword that.

When a sound is too loud, our automatic volume fader moves downward to make the sound quieter. In the same way you'd move a fader down with your finger if a lead/vocal was too loud in a mix, this is what a compressor does, only again it does it automatically.

But our automatic volume fader also does something else!

Using our vocal/lead example above, if you've pulled down the fader because the sound is too loud, then when it gets quiet again you'll move the fader back up so the volume of the sound stays level in the mix.

What this means is that when sounds become quiet again our automatic volume fader will simply return back to its original position.

So now that you've got some simple redefinitions of a regular compressor I'm going to redefine a multiband compressor, because it's really just a Dynamic EQ.

It's Not Multiband Compression, it's Dynamic EQing

I really look at a multiband compressor as a dynamic EQ, which is another way of saying an EQ on steroids.

In an EQ you have separate frequency bands that you can boost or cut. Boosting or cutting is exactly like moving a volume fader up or down for a given frequency band.

However **with an EQ the volume fader is static**. Once you set it, it stays.

In a multiband compressor that same volume fader can automatically move up and down in response to the loudness of the incoming signal. It does this without the need for your finger.

It's the ability of this fader to move up/down when it needs to without your finger that makes a multiband compressor a **Dynamic EQ.**

Dynamic EQing = Multiband Compression

Now the reason we refer to a multiband compressor as a Dynamic EQ is because unlike an EQ it doesn't always have to boost or cut from a given frequency band. This means that a 4-band multiband compressor has 4 automatic volume faders.

Let's look at what I mean when I say Dynamic because it's one of these ambiguous words, and so I want for you to know the two ways I'll be using it throughout this book:

1. Describing the difference in volume between loud and quiet parts
2. Describing the ability of a processor to adjust its behavior in response to the intensity of a signal.

Right now we're talking about the #2 definition above—the ability of a processor to adjust its behavior in response to the intensity of a signal. Let me give you an analogy to help that sink in better.

Cruise control in a car is dynamic.

If you set cruise control to 40/kmh and the speed drops down to 30/kmh the car will accelerate back up to 40/kmh. If the car reaches 50/kmh then the car will decelerate back down to 40/kmh. Cruise control is 'dynamically' responding and making adjustments to the speed of the car.

A multiband compressor is the same thing only it's dynamically increasing/decreasing the volume of a given frequency band based on how loud it is.

Cruise control dynamically changes speed, and a Dynamic EQ is dynamically changing its boost/cut in response to loudness.

Again when we say dynamic EQ we really just mean that the EQ can adjust itself relative to the incoming signal. As an example, with a regular EQ when you cut frequencies from a sound, it's going to always be removing that amount of volume for that specific frequency range. What this means is that:

An EQ is a <u>static</u> adjustment to the shape of the sound.

The limitation with EQ is that it's always boosting or cutting from the sound, no matter how loud it is in the frequency ranges you've set. So if for example you have a piano player hitting the keys hard then you might apply a -4db shelving cut at 1khz+ to remove some of that intense hammer pinging.

But what happens with that shelving cut when the player plays softly? Those softer pings will become even quieter, because the EQ is always reducing the volume of that range.

The EQ isn't reactive to the player himself. This is where multiband compression comes in because it's an EQ that doesn't have to subtract or add volume except for when you tell it to. This is why refer to it as an EQ on steroids.

There's something else I want you to know, no matter how ridiculously obvious it may seem.

Since each volume fader of a multiband compressor is capable of moving dynamically then it means it has two states:

1. Resting

2. Moving

When a volume fader is **resting** then nothing is happening to those frequencies aside from whatever level that fader is already at.

It's only once the threshold of the multiband compressor is exceeded that your volume fader will go from a **resting** state to a **moving** state.

So for a multiband compressor to work correctly, then the volume of the frequency band you're working on must change over time.

If the volume remains consistent, then there is no way for our automatic volume fader to go between **resting** and **moving** states.

So in order for a multiband compressor to act dynamically, the signal going into it must also be dynamic. This means some portion of its frequencies must be louder at one point and quieter at another point in time.

It took me forever to realize this, but multiband compressing sustain sounds like pads or a running oscillator is pointless because the sound stays pretty much the same in volume as it plays.

If the compressor triggers with a sustain sound it will always be on, continuously compressing and you will hear the sound of compression happening on your sustain instrument and it will mostly sound like shit.

Multiband Compression Controls Explained

Here's an explanation of all the controls you'll be using in a multiband compressor.

If you're already familiar with these then you can skip over them.

However, I would suggest at least understanding why I've grouped the controls into **Fader Triggering**, and **Fader Velocity** groups because it's an efficient way of dividing the controls of your compressor so that you can know where to do what.

Fader Triggering is comprised of the following 3 controls:

1. Threshold
2. Ratio
3. Sidechain

These controls tell our automatic volume fader **when** to move down, and **how much** volume to subtract when it does.

Fader Velocity is comprised of the following controls:

1. Attack
2. Hold

3. Release

These controls tell our automatic volume fader **how fast** it should move when the volume of the incoming sound is louder than your threshold setting.

Fader Triggering

The controls in this section allow our automatic volume fader to know **when** and **how much** to push down the volume of the incoming signal.

Threshold

Threshold tells the volume fader **when** to start decreasing the volume of our incoming signal. Sounds which extend above the level of our threshold cause our automatic volume fader to move down, thus decreasing the volume of our sound.

The threshold is the same thing as a height requirement for a theme park ride. If you're underneath the height threshold, then you don't get to ride the automatic volume fader down, but if you're above the height threshold then you're loud enough to go for a ride down in volume.

The threshold setting is responsible for letting a compressor know exactly **when to make a sound quieter**.

Signals which remain beneath our threshold cause our automatic volume fader to do absolutely nothing.

Ratio

Ratio is **how much** our automatic volume fader will move down when the volume of a sound extends above our threshold.

The higher our ratio, the more volume our fader will subtract when it is triggered.

The lower our ratio, the less volume our fader will subtract when it is triggered.

The difference between a high ratio and a low ratio is like the difference between gravity on earth vs. gravity on the moon. When you jump on earth you get pulled down right away, but when you jump on the moon, you go higher and you get pulled down slower and more gently.

It's the same with our ratio control. The lower our ratio, the more gently our volume fader pushes down. The higher the ratio the more aggressively our volume fader pushes down.

I'm avoiding the math behind how ratio works because I honestly forgot it even though it's really simple. I personally don't associate this math with the behavior of a compressor. In fact I largely attribute its existence to most of my confusion with figuring out how to use ratio effectively.

Higher ratios like 4:1 and 10:1 cause more gain reduction per db of threshold overshoot. Lower ratios like 1.5:1 and 2:1 cause less gain reduction per db of threshold overshoot. That's the math I can remember and in my head it's actually summed up as what follows.

The higher the ratio, the more gain-reduction. The lower the ratio, the less gain-reduction.

I could honestly care less about what amount of db is being subtracted per db of overshoot. It's so removed from what the ratio actually does in terms of shaping and aggressive behavior of the compressor that I find it virtually useless. Aggressiveness in music isn't a number, it's a sound—trust your ears.

In my opinion there are really only 3 ratio settings: 2:1, 4:1 and 10:1. When I'm configuring a compressor I always start at 2:1 and go straight to configuring the threshold/attack/release settings as they're the most important.

Fine tuning ratio isn't something you really do until you've figured out where you like your threshold, attack and release settings.

Sidechain

The Sidechain of a compressor is used to control how the compressor responds to the incoming signal.

A Sidechain's purpose is to allow the compressor to act as if it were behaving in response to an EQ'd version of the sound you're treating.

This is most often used to remove low frequencies from the incoming signal that's used to trigger the compressor.

It's useful because bass frequencies tend to last longer than high frequencies and so can cause compressors to respond more sluggishly and inconsistently.

What this means is that using a sidechain to remove low frequencies makes our compressor behave more precisely and predictably.

Gain Reduction

This isn't a control. But I've included it in this group, because it's the combination of threshold, ratio and sidechain settings which determines how much gain reduction a compressor will achieve.

As you're aware gain reduction is what a compressor does. Gain reduction means reducing the volume of a sound. So going back to our automatic volume fader, whenever a signal is louder than the threshold then compression is triggered and gain reduction occurs.

If ratio is kept the same, then the more a signal's volume goes over threshold, the more gain reduction you'll get.

It's exactly like if the louder a vocal got, the further you'd have to pull that fader down with your finger to get it to sit stably in the mix. If it was only slightly loud, you would just pull the fader down, very, very slightly.

I think I wondered this at some point, so in case you were wondering gain is the same thing as volume.

Fader Velocity

These controls tell our automatic volume fader **how fast** it should move when the volume of the incoming sound is louder than your threshold setting.

Attack

Attack is **how long** it takes our automatic volume fader to move downward when the threshold is exceeded by our incoming signal.

So for example, with a 10ms attack when our incoming signal exceeds the threshold of our compressor, it means that our automatic volume fader takes 10ms to decrease the volume as determined by our threshold and ratio controls.

Attack is the duration of travel for our automatic volume fader. It's the time it takes to travel from point A to point B. Point A is your fader at 0 gain reduction and point B is your fader at full gain reduction.

Once our attack is complete the volume fader will continue subtracting volume until the incoming signal gets quieter and falls beneath our threshold. Once this happens our automatic volume goes into the release phase.

Release

Release is **how long** it will take our automatic volume fader to return back to its original position of 0 volume reduction.

The release phase happens only once our incoming volume has fallen beneath the threshold we've selected.

So with a 10ms release, it would take our lowered automatic volume fader 10ms to return back to its original level of 0 volume reduction.

If as the compressor is completing its release timing the incoming signal goes back above the threshold, then the compressor will re-start its attack phase until gain reduction is achieved.

I know it might be redundant, but nobody ever explained what happens if your release isn't allowed to finish before the compressor is retriggered.

Hold

Hold is an extra parameter. Not all (multiband) compressors even have it because it isn't essential.

Hold actually happens before your release stage. **It's a way to delay the release phase** of our automatic volume fader.

So the order in which these stages happen is:

Attack > Hold > Release

As you're aware it's during the release stage that the fader makes the journey back to its original position of zero volume reduction.

When a sound gets quiet and falls beneath your threshold, the compressor would normally enter the release stage. But, with hold we are delaying the release stage from starting. The length of this delay is whatever length of time your hold setting is set to.

What this means is that during the hold phase we are maintaining our volume reduction at whatever point it's reached. Once hold completes, then the release stage goes into effect whereby our volume fader gradually returns to 0 volume reduction.

Other Controls

This is just an extra section to explain a few extra controls since they don't fit neatly with my Fader Triggering and Fader Velocity Groups.

Frequency Band

A multiband compressor allows you to independently select and treat frequency ranges with compression. As such the ranges of frequencies you'll be working with are interchangeably called frequency range/frequency band.

4-Zone Mix Theory is the most important thing to keep in mind when selecting your frequency ranges.

Understanding the value of setting each band to roughly operate somewhere within each zone will make your multiband compression decisions much more precise.

Makeup Gain

Since our automatic volume fader functions by reducing the volume of sounds, often the sounds we treat with compression can appear to become quieter.

Makeup Gain allows us to restore our instrument to its original perceived volume level.

However there will be many situations where you'll only be using compression to reduce the volume of a sound when it gets too loud.

This is because you're using the compressor as a peak controller whose only job is to viciously slap any overly loud sounds back into acceptable volume land. This is one of the easiest and most natural ways to use compression.

4-Zone Mix Theory

In order to know where to place the bands of a multiband compressor you need to understand 4-Zone Mix Theory.

It refers to the four main regions of sound we will be shaping and sculpting within our song. The reason it's valuable is because it's the easiest shortcut for quickly and effectively setting the correct frequency band within a multiband compressor.

What we want to do is have each frequency band configured so that it roughly operates within each of the 4 main frequency ranges I'm about to give you. By default every multiband processor is setup with these types of band divisions in mind because they are universally effective and sound extremely natural.

The 4 Zones

Lows: 0hz – 200hz

Bass and kick power as well as snare body located here. I often look at this as a specially reserved space for just my bass/kick power—snare gets a free pass. Everything else should be aggressively removed/diminished within this range.

Mids: 200hz – 1khz

The meat and body of most instruments lies in this range. It's important to be very selective about which instruments you allow to be dominant within this range or else you'll get a muddy mix.

High Mids: 1khz – 7khz

This is where the forwardness and presence of your instruments reside. This is our ears most sensitive range (in particular our ear is most sensitive to boosts and cuts @ 2 - 3khz).

Highs: 7khz – 20khz

Cymbals and hi-hats are very dominant in this range. This is where the Sizzle, Aliveness, and High-Definition quality of our instruments comes from. If the mix is too sibilant, or airy sounding this is the range too look at.

Understanding 4-Zone Mix Theory allows us to break down our mix into 4 frequency-dependent zones. We can then use multiband compression to work with just the instruments that occupy a problematic frequency range as we improve the clarity of our mix.

As you'll discover later on, by just setting up your frequency bands to roughly match these ranges, you'll have a much easier time exploring the benefits multi-band compression.

If you want to begin shaping a frequency range, but aren't sure where to set your crossovers simply refer to this section and you'll have a very good place to start. I use these ranges all the time, they're spectacular.

32 | MASTERING MULTI-BAND COMPRESSION

Blend/Contrast Theory and Multiband Compression

If you've read any of my other books then you know that the foundation of my mixing philosophy is **blend** and **contrast**. I want for 70% of my instruments to blend together into the background of my mix, and the other 30% to contrast and push forward into the front of my mix.

By following this rule I'm able to create massive depth with less effort and less stress.

I can assure you, within a few sessions of applying this paradigm it will transform the way you approach mixing. You'll be more exacting with your decisions and you won't find yourself getting stuck debating whether something is right or wrong.

All you need to do is decide if an instrument is **blending** or **contrasting**.

At every level of my mixing, this is my primary goal. Why do I use *The 3-Space Reverb Framework* when mixing? Because it's sonically designed to create more **blend** and **contrast**.

Why do I rely on 4-Zone Mix theory in *The EQ and Compression Formula* Because in each of the 4 frequency zones I always make sure there's 1 instrument that's louder (**contrasting**) and the rest are just supporting (**blending**).

How specifically am I using Bus Compression in *The Bus Compression Framework*? I'm using it to create improved **blending** via the glue effect of bus compression. But I'm also using it to create more **contrast** by pushing instrument groups apart. We do this by applying numerically contrasting compression settings to each group.

What this means is that a **contrasting** instrument group will always have more open compression settings compared to a **blending** instrument group which has more restrictive compression settings.

It's the additive effect of these precise and repeatable techniques which creates increasing levels of blend/contrast. With increasing levels of blend/contrast we make massive depth and crystal clarity an effortless byproduct of a formulaic mixing methodology.

This is what I aim for when I teach this stuff.

Can you make someone a great mixer right away? No, but you can teach them the exact sequences and patterns that great mixers use.

Unfortunately many great artists and mixers aren't exactly aware of how they do what they do and I think that's bullshit because it holds the rest of us back. It makes those of us just starting think the learning curve is steep.

It isn't as steep as we think. It's the time investment that's steep. But that's the price for anything worth having.

So everything I talk about is a formula. It's a methodology that you can copy and paste into your process to get an instant skip over the confusion.

We really need to experience results that we can appreciate in order to connect the deeper dots--the ones we're really after.

So knowing whether I'm after **blend** or **contrast** is my deeper connecting of the dots. It lets me know exactly what to do so that I don't get lost trying to figure out what I'm after. It's very simple and at the same time, this way of mixing isn't so rigid or encumbering that it drops me from a creative state.

Blend/contrast is a universal of art. Our perceptions are built around it. Hot-cold, black-white, happy-sad, quiet-loud, distant-close—everything.

So when we're mixing it's all about intensifying blend/contrast and the way we do this with multiband compression has to do with the 2 main results Multiband Compression can achieve. They are as follows:

1. **Transient Control**
    a. **Transient Enhancement**
    b. **Transient Reduction**
2. **Volume Leveling**

These 2 results also happen to be the exact same ways we use a regular compressor.

The only difference is that now we can do it on a specific frequency range which is what gives us the ability to use a multiband compressor to flexibly shape the frequency content of a sound.

Again, you can only shape a given frequency range if it has differences in volume to work with. If it's always sustaining at the same general volume, then multiband compression has virtually no positive benefit worth confusing ourselves with.

Transient Control for Blend/Contrast

Transient in the context of a multiband compressor means shaping the peak volume of a frequency range. Now the sentence I just said is true, but it can be super vague so don't worry if it doesn't make sense yet, because the first 2 multiband compression techniques I'm going to give you will show you exactly how to achieve transient control.

For the most part it is going to be the results that connect the dots. The 17 techniques I'm going to be showing you a little later will give you the exact results you need to figure things out.

Examples are almost always clearer than the technical explanations. Technical explanations are just meant to prime your mind so that you're a little more subconsciously prepared to connect the dots when you get a demonstration later on.

So as a quick review here's exactly what I mean about transient control as it relates to **blend** vs. **contrast**:

1. **Transient Enhancement will always = More Contrast**
2. **Transient Reduction will always = More Blend**

Volume Leveling for Blend/Contrast

Volume leveling in the context of a multiband compressor means reducing the difference between loud and quiet portions of a given frequency range.

In our earlier example with the piano hammer playing louder and then quieter, we can set compression to reduce the volume of just the loud part so it gets closer in volume to the quiet part. Then simply applying makeup gain brings the overall level of volume back up, hence **volume leveling**.

Whenever a given frequency range gets too loud it begins to contrast and move toward the front of our mix. When it gets too quiet it can overly blend and eventually disappear into the background of our mix.

So we volume level frequency ranges because sometimes they're too loud and sometimes they're too quiet and leveling out the volume level makes that frequency range sit more stably in your mix.

Generally in mixes you want the majority of instruments to remain fairly dynamically stable because this gives you control over their mix placement.

But mixing is an art, and sometimes having 1 or 2 instruments be able to dynamically warp in and out of your mix because of their dramatic changes in volume can create more contrast and depth.

As you'll learn in the techniques I'm going to show you, much of the time we simply reduce the volume of loud parts without applying makeup gain. This is something that's counterintuitive because makeup gain is sort of presented as the final step of using any compressor and so some people assume it's meant to be used all the time—it's not, I'm going to show and explain why later on.

Volume Leveling is primarily a **blend** effect, simply because it holds stuff in place. But you can also hold stuff in place so it's louder and more present and in this way it becomes more of a **contrast effect.**

With volume leveling we are using the multiband compressor to prevent individual frequency ranges from darting back and forth throughout our mix.

You'll get a perfect example of **volume leveling** frequencies that move back and forth in your mix with technique #3. In that technique I'll show you the very visual example of how to control resonantly sweeping frequencies in your mix.

In fact, the reason volume leveling is so effective when dealing with sweeping resonances is because sometimes we like lots of resonance, but it can be overwhelming in certain frequency ranges and so wont fit perfectly with the mix. Volume leveling with multiband compression is the ultimate solution to this problem.

The techniques you're going to learn are the ones I use. Because it's me, they are incredibly formulaic and they work.

I'm giving them to you, partly because I feel obligated since I know I'm not the only one who was, for the longest time, ruthlessly tortured by multiband compression at a CIA blacksite called my studio.

I only want for you to find out for yourself just how effective the techniques are because they're going to free up a lot of mental energy so you can eventually focus on more important decisions like **blend** and **contrast**.

The more we don't have to think about **how** to use something and the more we can just fiddle with a tool while aiming for something simple like "**is it blending or contrasting?**" the more it becomes an enjoyable exploration and the more creativity blossoms.

I'm telling you this because multiband compression is one of the most creatively inhibiting tools to learn. It's so freaking technical if you don't have simple ways of approaching it.

If you look it at it like it's this multi-layered, inter-dimensional mixing behemoth of a tool, then it will own you.

Don't Aim for Perfection, Aim for Good Enough

I wasn't going to include this section because it felt off topic, but then I remembered you bought a book on multiband compression.

It's time we jump into some applied psychology, because this is something I'm big about. All forms of art are intensely psychological; there are mechanisms at play that will forever remain beyond your control. That being said, in this section I want to give you an awareness of a particular trap many mixers fall into.

It doesn't just relate to music, it has to do with any time a person finds themselves in a problem/obsessive loop state. It doesn't happen to everyone, but it's more likely to happen to people who have a very strong belief that they can achieve their idea of perfection.

First and foremost, perfection isn't real. It's a subjective experience. What's perfect one day, you'll eventually find something wrong with. So it's much better to aim for what's **Good Enough** instead of what's perfect. When it's good enough you can always improve. Once it's perfect, it can only go down-hill from there. This is a weird quirk of perception.

Perfectionism is a mindfuck that has largely been trained into us by a deluge of ego-based narratives and desperate attempts to exert control in a world where we really have limited control.

Go on social media and you're walking into an art gallery of the most perfectly curated content there is. People who can't even say a complete and engaging sentence to save their lives, chop up a video so it has rhythm, punctuation, and timing. All the things they lack. It's like the early 2000s vocal trance of vlogging. Chop chop chop, "Wow I've never experienced this before. How cool!!!"

The world is mostly just everyone presenting the ideation of who they want you to think they are. There's nothing wrong with this, identity is a function of life. But all the fun identities are a function of art. That's why the guy who can't even say a complete sentence can suddenly chop up a video where he's the Tony Robbins of vlogging. I wonder how many takes it took him to get that delivery perfect? Even world class actors need multiple takes.

Anyway, there are a million possible incremental changes you could make to a sound with a multiband compressor. You could get lost if you think incremental changes make a big difference, because they don't, that's why they're incremental. Instead you want broad, sweeping changes that are easy to tell the difference between.

If you go the opposite route, you're going to create what I call **expectation-tension** in your body as you go looking for "problems that must be there." Well of course they must be there, you created the expectation that they are and so you go searching.

The tension part is the dangerous part, because this is what gets people stuck in loops. The tension is the body-feeling part of the behavior, it's the part that propels it and maintains it. It's a venomous combination of negative muscular tension and inhibited breathing that usually remains just beneath our conscious awareness.

We're generally aware when there is a problem, but we're usually not aware of the body-feeling that's driving it.

Negative muscular-body tension is a negative feeling and feelings are always attached to what is most contextually relevant to them. So if you're looking for something and know it's a problem; that usually starts up tension in the body *because it's a problem*.

The majority of people respond to problems by creating tension in their body. That's a big part of how they know it's a problem, because it feels like one.

Anyway what's dangerous is the longer you spend with that tension the more it looks to perpetuates itself and when you do eventually solve the 1st problem, you'll often find yourself looking for another problem that isn't there.

Was it really your choice at that point? No it wasn't, the feeling continues to direct your thoughts even after you solved the initial problem that created it. And because thoughts are always contextualized to the way you feel, your thoughts will re-contextualize to a new problem in order to loop into and support your feelings. It's a biological feedback loop, and since this is a book for mixers and I know we're a very particular bunch—I know that for a good chunk of us this happens somewhere along the way and it's generally not fun.

We're not as motivated if we don't feel anything. That's just how it works. You can be motivated for problems or motivated for solutions. I'm trying to help you become aware of a problem so that you can catch it and at least have the choice rather than a compulsion.

Just be aware that if you get caught in a loop, there's a feeling that's propelling and maintaining it. You have a few choices to avoid this:

1. Get up from your chair, take a 5minute break. Go move somewhere else. As soon as you get back go somewhere else in your project.
2. Consciously decide to go elsewhere so you don't have to take a break
3. Take a moment and find where the muscle tension is in your body. It can be in the shoulders, neck or the belly and release it and move on. At first you have to constantly manage releasing muscle tension or it just comes back and puts you in the same state. So for some people this isn't easy to do at first. This is basically what people learn to do with meditation and why they love it. I love it because it feels like I'm on a cosmic rainbow wave of awesomeness.
4. I'm not even that good at #3, if you watch my production videos I rely on speed and constantly moving from place to place very quickly to avoid falling into loops. So technique #4 is just moving so haphazardly fast that you don't really have time for your mind to catch problems.

So why am I going deep into this psychological phenomenon in this book? Because we're talking about multi-mother-f*#king-band compression, the most nebulous, nefarious, unintentionally obfuscated, problem inducing processor there is. It's caused all of us problems, no one is given mercy. You either learn it or you'll avoid it.

I've met many mixers that get caught in this negative loop, and so I felt obligated to at least talk about it because I've seen how quickly it drops people from flow and creativity. It's the boogeyman of creativity.

Where to Use Multiband Compression

Before we get into the nitty gritty, I have to talk about where we typically use Multiband compression.

Multiband compression can be used on single tracks, instrument groups (buses), and the master. This book is mostly about using multiband compression on the individual and group level of projects because those are the most effective and cleanest place to use it.

The reason for that is because multiband compressing a master is the easiest way to ruin your track. Multiband compressing at the individual track or group level is actually what gives you the most control over your entire mix, and it leads to the best mixes.

That being said in technique #17 I will be showing you how I personally approach multiband compression on my master, because I think it's one of the cleanest, most transparent ways to use a multiband compressor on the master. It's my favorite way to use multiband compression because it's subtractive in nature and that makes it extremely transparent and clean.

17 Powerful Multiband Compression Techniques

As former gamers, my friends and I like to call important levels of personal development Raids. A raid is a boss fight. Before we go into this boss battle of multiband compression together, I want to give you some tips about learning.

We're not about to Leeroy Jenkins this sh*t. I'm giving you the cheat codes because this is real life and getting stomped by a boss is annoying. We want to win so let's show you how.

To begin I would suggest that as you read through these techniques that you test them out within a session. The rest of this book is simply a reference manual for how to deploy multiband compression.

Please feel free to reread and experiment with these 17 techniques as much as you need to.

In fact I'll say what I wouldn't have said years ago, because the 17 techniques you'll be learning are really just multiband compression presets. But they're better than just presets because you get the added bonus of my sometimes electric explanations for how they work and how you can use them.

I can't tell you how to learn other than to say that the learning school teaches us isn't as relevant to learning in the real world. Yes some of the skills transfer over, but the idea of cramming everything into your head at the same time and really grasping it doesn't translate to actually deploying those skillsets to achieve actual results.

We should be learning through action, not memorization, memorization is a byproduct of action and very short 1 - 3 minute instances of thinking about what you learned. As you review some of what you learned it's healthy to imagine how you might apply it again even if you don't fully understand it yet. This starts to create the grooves in your mind where learning automatically happens.

By beginning to build the grooves in your nervous system that say "I'm learning about this topic." Eventually your brain just connects the dots and when you're finally ready, it will just happen--you'll just get it.

Don't worry about what you don't know, that only inhibits the effectiveness of learning. The process of not knowing, and being curious about your not knowing is ½ the process of learning. Worrying and getting anxious about not knowing only inhibits learning, this is something schooling has unfortunately strongly reinforced in some people.

Anyway that's my magnum opus on learning:

1. Be ok with not knowing everything
2. Short instances of applying a single skill 10 - 20 minutes.
3. Take a 5 minute break— do something unrelated. (**actually the most important step after applying a new skill you really want to learn**)
4. Rinse Repeat

I should tell you I don't fine tune so much as I swing knobs to 2 or 3 major positions and listen for which one I like the most.

I believe a big part of mixing and music is happy accidents, and there ain't no way you're going to have nearly as many happy accidents when you're slugging your way through an infinite number of slightly different settings that are incredibly hard for anybody to notice unless they hallucinate a difference. A lot of budding mixers go through the phase of hallucinating the benefit of minor adjustments—but the answer isn't really there.

A quick swing of a knob through 1 or 2, (maybe 3) choices will very quickly let you know what range you prefer to have it in. Once you know the range you like then you can fine tune to your heart's content.

With each technique I will do my best to explain what's important, while keeping each explanation as concise as possible. That being said, I repeat certain concepts and ideas because learning is the result of repetition.

Also you will notice that a good amount of the techniques rely on 1 or 2 bands. This is because it's the easiest way to learn multiband compression. It's also because the techniques that rely on 1 or 2 bands can eventually be combined together to achieve a more complex techniques.

Obviously it's easier to learn one simple technique at a time and then combine them together for your needs, so that is the way I've presented it.

As a quick refresher a compressor only achieves two things:

1. **Transient Control**
    a. Transient Enhancement
    b. Transient Reduction
2. **Volume Leveling**
    a. Keeping volume levels within a consistent range so they sit better in the mix.

A multiband compressor allows us to do those exact jobs, but on a per frequency band basis. This means you'll notice many of the techniques I show you are just using the multiband compressor to focus on the fewest frequency ranges needed to get the job done.

Techniques 1 - 2 will show you how to achieve **Transient Control**

Techniques 2 - 3 will demonstrate **Volume Leveling**.

Techniques 4 – 17 will be some mixture of the two.

So it's finally time! Let's wreck this boss.

(1 – 2) Transient Control Techniques

#1
Transient Enhancement of Plucky Sounds
(Guitars, Pianos, Plucky Synths)

This is a very simple technique because it's exactly like using a transient shaper only it's more precise and you can use it on a variety of instruments. The goal is of course to enhance the attack of an instrument. Test this on a piano—it's the easiest way to experience it.

1. Set a Frequency Band from 1khz – 20khz on the desired instrument.
2. Set Attack 20ms.
3. Set Release 20ms.
4. Set Ratio 2:1.
5. Set Makeup Gain +6db.
6. Bring threshold down until you get 4 - 6db of reduction.

When I say makeup gain +6db that means that our volume fader is adding +6db to that frequency range. This is important because when a gain reduction of -6db takes place, it means our volume fader has moved down from +6db back to 0db, which effectively cancels your makeup gain.

Makeup gain in a multiband compressor is effectively just an EQ boost or cut control until compression takes place. This is how I think of it.

What you'll notice as you bring that threshold down is that a portion of the initial 6db boost is actually shaped away as our automatic volume fader moves down. This downward movement is reflected by the gain reduction meter in your multiband compressor.

The 20ms attack is how long it takes the volume fader to move all the way down to the desired gain reduction. This is exactly like the decay envelope on an ADSR envelope for a synthesizer.

This is really cool because it means you get to control when and for how long that 1khz+ boost operates for. The longer your attack, the longer the boost. The shorter your attack the shorter your boost.

The release only takes place once that frequency band's volume falls beneath your threshold. Once that happens, in our example it takes 20ms for your volume fader to return back to your makeup gain of +6db.

When it comes to fine tuning the shape of your transient like this, I always start with the make-up gain boost because it's literally being used just like an EQ at the beginning.

Then I set the attack and release at the aforementioned settings and ratio at 2:1 and **the magic happens when I bring that threshold down**. The act of bringing that threshold down actuates the dynamic EQ shaping process.

Once you've got your threshold where you like it, you can fiddle with the attack and release settings to see how you might like to further shape your sound. Higher ratios will make the snap of the compressor more noticeable, but will also make the attack increasingly have less body and become more of a 'pop' sound.

As I've already mentioned, there's really only 3 ratio settings:

1. 2:1 (**Transparent**)
2. 4:1 (**Aggressive**)
3. 10:1 (**Ultra Aggressive**).

Using 10:1 ratios for this technique is not uncommon and can be very desirable.

It's also not uncommon for me to follow the transient enhancing multiband compressor with a limiter when using this technique. This allows me to control the new peakiness I've created in the sound. The limiter should be shaving off anywhere from 1 - 5db. This is only necessary if you find your new transient peak is wreaking havoc on your mix or master limiter.

In this particular example with the piano I would very unlikely feel the need to limit it. But if we were doing the same technique with a kick transient then there's a much greater chance of needing to control the peak created by this treatment.

#2
Transient Reduction of Plucky Sounds
(Guitars, Pianos, Plucky Synths)

This is just the reverse of the technique I showed you. We use this to selectively reduce the transient information in a given frequency so in this case the transient information 1khz+.

Sometimes you'll have a plucky instrument that sounds great by itself but then in the mix it's too pokey and when you use a regular single band compressor to get rid of the attack it sucks away its body and suffocates it. A selective band at 1khz+ solves this. Here's how.

1. Set a Frequency Band from 1khz – 20khz on the desired instrument.
2. Set Attack 0ms.
3. Set Release 20ms.
4. Set Ratio 2:1.
5. Bring Threshold down until the transient disappears just a little more than necessary.

Once you push the transient back just a bit more than you need to, go back to your attack and start to open it to around 2 - 10ms. This will restore some of the transient information.

There is no makeup gain here because we are cutting frequency energy that is already there. Conversely in the technique before this we were trying to add energy/volume that wasn't there.

With this technique you have complete control over the duration and intensity of any transient. Attack controls duration and bringing the threshold down decreases intensity.

In other words, with this technique, threshold is a lot more like an EQ cut, and attack is the time-shape of that EQ cut—how long it takes that EQ cut to go into full effect.

These first two techniques are probably about 30% of my multiband compression use.

Sometimes you'll find that the transient information really begins at a frequency higher than 1khz, maybe 2khz - 5khz. You can figure this out by just soloing your frequency band and dragging it across as you listen for where the transient mainly sits.

Simply set the crossover around those frequencies. Where you set crossover is really just a preference, but you'll be surprised just how often a crossover will sit right near the range points of our 4-Zone Mix Theory.

That's because it's natural to the ear and it's natural for mixing.

All the confusion about where to place crossovers could be avoided by generally positioning them near the frequency boundaries of 4-Zone Mix Theory. That's how I do it.

(3 - 4) Volume Leveling

Before I show you these volume leveling techniques I want to explain volume leveling a little more because I think it will help you better understand what we're achieving.

I'm going to be showing you **how to level the volume level of individual frequency bands.**

When I say 'leveling individual frequency bands' I mean a situation in which a specific frequency band's volume changes to such a degree that it goes in and out of balance with your mix. When I say out of balance here, it means that it either pokes out (**too loud**) or disappears (**too quiet**) in your mix.

Examples of instruments that typically need this treatment are instruments that are played by musicians: Guitars, Pianos as well as Synths. The most obvious case is dynamic synths like growl basses and synths that automate a lot.

Again, when I say dynamic, I mean the volume in a given frequency band just changes a bunch. Sometimes it's loud, sometimes it's quiet which causes it to poke out or disappear in a mix. This can

be undesirable when trying to keep instruments in fixed positions.

Let's explain why volume leveling individual frequency bands is so beneficial.

The main issue we're dealing with is that frequency balance in the sound isn't consistent. With a piano player when they play forcefully, the sound of the hammer hitting the piano string might be too loud, but when they play softly it sounds fine.

With an EQ you could apply a shelving cut at 1khz+ to decrease the intensity of the hammer, but then when the piano is played softly, the sound of the hammer hitting the string would also be diminished and likely disappear in your mix. Unfortunately, a static EQ isn't equipped for this job.

You need a dynamic EQ that cuts when the ping sound is too loud and leaves those 1khz+ frequencies unaffected when the keys are pressed softly. This is exactly what multiband compression was designed for.

Any time a given frequency range is inconsistent, which means it gets too loud at times and other times it's too quiet, this is what multiband compression is suited for.

For the most part, the majority of sounds are consistent enough in terms of frequency intensity over time. But as you'll discover through the rest of this book, things like vocals, acoustic instruments, and dynamically evolving synths like growl basses or anything with a sweeping resonant peak can cause frequency balance issues as they evolve over time.

It's a lot like being at the beach and sitting a few feet from where the water meets the shore and it's great. But then the tide creeps up and you can't sit there anymore or you get wet.

Compression prevents the tides of volume from changing so you can comfortably sit an instrument on whatever shore you want.

You could use a single band compressor to fix that issue, but again, a regular compressor doesn't let you shape the frequency balance of sound to fit with everything else. Instead a single band compressor literally just glues the volume of the entire sound in place.

Conversely, a multiband compressor lets you fix a specific frequency bands volume in place. Since you can setup a frequency band in whatever range(s) you want, the surgical application of volume leveling and shaping is incredibly flexible.

Now let's start by learning how to volume level Sweeping Resonant Peaks because it's a dramatic example of controlling frequency peaks with multiband compression.

#3
Controlling Sweeping Resonant Peaks

In electronic music styles it's very common to have a very resonant peak filter sweeping across a sound. The acid sounds of tb-303's are known for this.

One of the main issues when working with sounds like this is that as the resonance slides across the frequency range it moves from weaker to stronger parts of our hearing. This means that at times the sound could fit perfectly but at others it sticks out like a sore thumb.

If you've ever had trouble getting an instrument with resonance sweeping to sit in your mix, then this is the ultimate solution.

It's best if you can see the frequencies on a spectrum analyzer as you do this. It will help you to set the appropriate frequency range for compression.

1. Play an instrument with a sweeping and very resonant filter. (You'll see the resonant peak sweeping across the frequency spectrum on the spectrum analyzer). As it sweeps notice where it begins to stick out in your mix. Wherever it starts and wherever it ends will be the boundaries of your compression band.
2. Set Attack 20ms.

3. Set Release 20ms.
4. Set Ratio 2:1.
5. Bring Threshold down until you get enough gain reduction to prevent the offending resonant frequency range from poking out in your mix.

I often find that the offending frequency band is usually 800hz - 7khz. It's not surprising because our hearing is most sensitive in this range.

Sometimes you'll need more than one band because you find that one type of gain reduction across the entire range of resonance decreases it too much at times and just right at others.

This is where the effectiveness and flexibility of multiband compression comes into play.

#4
Controlling Frequency Peaks at the Group/Bus Level

The resonant peak compression example we did above is the exact same thing as this. It's just a much more dramatic example.

In this scenario you're still dealing with peaks, only now the peaks are the result of multiple instruments layering together. This won't always be as visually obvious on a spectrum analyzer, so you have to use your ears.

Anyway, so as instruments are playing together within a group they layer and as such begin to build resonances in certain frequency ranges where their energies meet.

Whereas by themselves they play fine in more sparse areas of your track, very often at the chorus when everything comes together they add together and create resonances or 'frequency imbalances' in certain frequency ranges.

We use multiband compression at the group level to fix this.

An example of this would be a synth group that's meant to play behind and support a lead vocal. The synth group may contain pads, chords, piano's, and perhaps even some plucky synths.

You might discover that occasionally this group has an undesirable increase in frequency intensity somewhere between 800khz - 5khz which is the primary range for intelligibility of the vocalist and most lead instruments.

Now normally you can just do an EQ dip in this range and it solves the problem. But sometimes it already sounds perfect it's just at specific parts of a vocal phrase where melodies of the pads/keys come together that you get these peaks and they overwhelm the vocalist. This is where multiband compression comes in handy. Here's how:

1. Put the Multiband Compressor on the group.
2. Set just one Frequency Band at 800hz – 5khz.
3. Set Attack to 10ms.
4. Set Release to 20 - 30ms.
5. Set Ratio to 2:1.
6. As the entire mix plays, bring the Threshold down until it catches the specific parts where the volume builds up in that frequency range and swamps your lead instrument.

17 Powerful Multiband Compression Techniques | 71

You'll notice as you bring the threshold down that it very gently subdues the forwardness of the instrument group that's conflicting with your vocal/lead.

Now the idea is to catch just the loud parts happening in that frequency range, but you could bring the threshold down a bit further so the range is always being reduced in its average volume.

If you bring the range down like this, then you'll be more aggressively pushing back any frequency intensity in this range which will create greater separation between your vocals/leads and supporting instruments.

What's really fun about this technique is you get to hear it in the context of your mix. This is how I do it.

I have very ballpark numbers for beginning the configuration of a multiband compressor and they are a kind of one-size-fits-all and so they allow me to focus on just getting within arm's reach of the sound I'm after.

Once I'm in range. I go back and fine tune things like attack, and release and ratio.

At this point you've essentially learned everything you'll ever do with a multiband compressor: **Transient Control** and **Volume Leveling**.

The rest of the techniques are just variations of volume leveling and transient control but for different instruments and in some more complex and powerful ways.

(5 – 17) Collection of Techniques

#5
Shaping Snare Body

The body of a snare is generally located in the 200hz range. This is where you'll see a bump on a spectrum analyzer. Typically we boost this with EQ. The weakness with EQ boosting is that it can't be done too heavily or the snare gets a kind of undesirable boominess.

You can do the same thing with a multiband compressor, but it allows you to control for exactly how long that range is boosted which means you can shape the body of the snare exactly as you want. Here's how you do it.

1. Set a Frequency Band 100hz - 300hz, or just so the frequency band is center on the snare bump you see on a spectrum analyzer.
2. Set the Attack to 30ms.
3. Set the Release to 30ms.
4. Set the Ratio to 2:1.

5. Add Makeup Gain until you get the fullness and body you want.
6. Now bring the Threshold down until you like the body shape you've got.

For me it's typically around 3db of boost with 3 - 4db of gain reduction. This literally gives the body of your snare more punch, since that's what the compression is doing—it's punching down on the frequency body of the snare.

You can open/close your attack depending on how long you want that body boost to stay audible. The more open your attack more the more body your snare gets, the more closed your attack the more snappy the body gets—almost like a pop.

You can experiment with higher ratios to get more aggressive snappiness.

What really helps to understand this effect is that before you actuate any compression you first EQ boost (makeup gain) the sound. This makes it really obvious what you're 'compressing away' as you bring the threshold down.

Bringing the threshold down causes the compressor to be actuated by the incoming signal and so your automatic volume fader will then slide down and shape the volume of that frequency band.

#6
Shaping Snare Snap

Shaping the snap of a snare is very easy to do. Normally I find the snappiness of a snare to be a combination of shaping the body as we just discussed in #5 and also applying transient shaping to the 5khz + frequency ranges. Here's how:

1. Set a Frequency Band to between 5khz – 20khz.
2. Set Attack to 15ms.
3. Set Release to 20ms.
4. Set Ratio 4:1.
5. Add 2 - 4db of makeup gain, just like you're EQ boosting the high frequency content of the sound.
6. Bring the Threshold down until you get 2 - 4db of compression.

As you're already familiar, whenever we're doing **transient enhancement**, we're aiming for about as much gain reduction as we added with the make-up gain. This isn't always the case but it's a risk-free starting point when shaping the transient of a sound.

#7
Adding Kick Punch

With kicks it's often difficult to get the punch you want them to have. When I say punch in particular I mean the frequency content between 80hz and 150hz. It's somewhat of a weird place to do a constant boost with an EQ, unless it's very gentle. So a multiband compressor would be better at doing more aggressive shaping of lower frequencies like this. Here's how:

1. Set a Frequency Band 80hz - 120hz.
2. Set Attack 20ms.
3. Set Release 30ms.
4. Set Ratio 2:1 or 4:1 depending on the desired aggressiveness of the effect.
5. Add 1 - 6db Makeup Gain depending on how much punch you'd like to have.
6. Bring the Threshold down until you get the sound you want or you've got 1 - 6db of gain reduction.

With gain reduction I'm aiming for almost equal to whatever amount of makeup gain I applied. So if I added 3db of makeup gain, I'll likely aim for 2-3db of gain reduction.

This is a surprisingly effective way to reshape a kick's punch. If the punch is already there and you just want to boost it 1 - 2db then an EQ will usually be fine. But if you want to add a more dramatic amount of punch to the kick multiband compression will do a better job.

#8
Removing Kick Woofiness

You'll often have a great kick with a great attack and a great sub but it's really 'woofy'.

As you may be aware, woofiness lives in the 120hz - 800hz range. Unfortunately, aggressive EQ cutting between 150hz - 800hz to remove woofiness has the tendency to suck some of the life out of your kick. Enter Dynamic EQing.

1. Set Frequency Band somewhere between 150hz - 800hz.
    a. You can find the problem frequencies faster by bringing the makeup gain of that band down -6db and then sliding the band left to right until you get the biggest improvement. Reset the gain to 0 when you've found your range.
2. Set Attack to 15ms.
3. Set Release to 20ms.
4. Set Ratio 2:1.
5. Bring the Threshold down until you get whatever amount of gain reduction makes your kick sound the best.

We aren't applying any makeup gain because we are simply subtracting the woofy frequency range.

As with many of the other techniques, it's not until you move the threshold down that you'll get the shape of the sound you want. The threshold is essentially your big control knob; it's the one you turn to get the desired effect.

Keep in mind, that with all these techniques, once you've got your threshold where you like, you can always go back through your attack, release and ratio settings to tweak them to your heart's content.

I think it's much more reliable to aim to get your sound just within range of what you want. It doesn't need to be perfect. I say this because there are a million possible settings and trust me when I say that if you use the techniques in this book you'll avoid 80% of the tweaking trouble and quickly and consistently get what you're after.

We've mainly been working with simpler single-band and sometimes two-band multiband compression so far because these are not only the easiest but also the most common ways that multiband compression is used.

I personally use 1 – 2 bands about 80% of the time and 20% of the time I use 3 - 4. So there's a huge difference

17 Powerful Multiband Compression Techniques | 81

and unfortunately many producers/engineers fall into the trap of thinking they need all 4.

#9
Strengthening the Body of a Sound
(Acoustic Guitars, Piano, Organic Sounds)

If you have an instrument where you feel the body disappears at times, or it just isn't playing loud enough then this technique is perfect for you.

This trick will add more midrange to whatever you apply it to which is why it's good for acoustic guitars that lack body because of mic distance/placement/etc. So here goes:

1. Set Frequency Band to 120hz – 600hz.
2. Set Attack 20ms.
3. Set Release 30ms.
4. Set Ratio 2:1.
5. Add 1 - 4db of Makeup Gain.
6. Now bring the Threshold down until you get about 2 -3 db of gain reduction.

We start by bringing up the makeup gain and at this point the multiband compressor is nothing more than an EQ. As usual what you'll notice as you bring that threshold down is the body is given more shape.

How long you want initial attack of the instrument to be boosted depends on the length of your attack. The longer your attack the longer the boost will happen for. If you wanted to shape the body less and just have an overall longer boost to the body then you could jump into 100 – 200ms attack territory.

#10
Compressing Sub Frequencies for More Power

Sometimes the low end of your mix can be very dynamic. Big changes in volume with your low bass frequencies are somewhat likely to wreak havoc on the behavior of your limiter when it comes time to master.

This happens because in terms of a whole mix, bass contains the most volume energy.

Master Channel Limiters don't have fun trying to track dynamics in bass, they just don't. They've got the whole entire frequency range to work on so we want to have the volume differences in our bass as controlled as possible before they hit the limiter.

Now when I say volume differences I mean the difference in volume between when it's just your kick hitting, and when your kick and bass hit together.

As an example when your kick hits alone you might get a peak volume of -6db, but then when you're kick and bass hit together you get a peak volume of -3db. This is the difference in volume we want to take care of before our bass hits the limiter. We don't have to completely remove the entire difference, but we just want to touch it up a little bit.

Good individual track EQing and Sidechaining can mitigate most of the issues here, but it still won't completely handle all the peak volume created by the bass and kick happening together.

So what we're going to do is show you how to reduce this peak sub energy to allow for a cleaner master limiting process.

The benefit of this is that it will happen without dramatically affecting the balance of your mix. In fact you should expect to lose a little sub energy, but it will actually lead to a punchier and louder mix by saving some headroom.

This technique is typically done on the master channel of your mix. Here's how:

1. Set a Frequency Band from 0hz – 150hz.
2. Set Attack to 30ms.
3. Set Release to 30ms.
4. Set Ratio 2:1.
5. Bring Threshold down until it only triggers 1 - 3 db of compression when your kick and bass hit at the same time before.

If it triggers a little gain reduction before the kick and bass double up, that's fine. The idea is to just have the majority of the gain reduction happening when they both double up.

This will give you more headroom which is really just a way of saying that because it's reducing peak volume in your mix it allows you to apply more limiting, simply because your limiter isn't getting hit as hard.

This particular technique brings you closer to the mastering utopia of everything hitting the limiter at about the same time. Usually your kick and snare are problematic in this regard. They tend to hit the limiter days before anything else gets close to it, and as a result they drive the behavior and response of the limiter.

You'll get anywhere from 1 - 3db of gain reduction if your mix was solid to begin with. Anything beyond this is usually remedial work and generally requires more involved mastering type solutions.

#11
Multiband Compressing for Increased Front/Back Depth

In all my books I stress the importance of **Front** to **Back** Mixing. Front to back mixing is the same exact thing as **contrast** and **blend**. In that order, so you have:

Front = Contrast

Back = Blend

Instruments that **blend** are perceived as being in the back of your mix. Anything that contrasts with the back is perceived as being in the **front**, that's why it's contrasting.

It's important to understand this in order to know what you're mixing decisions are moving towards, otherwise your mixes will sound flat and lifeless.

In the context of multiband compression, **Front** to **Back** depth is achieved whenever a given frequency range is dynamically shaped so it sits either more in the front or more in the back of your mix.

With **Transient Enhancement** you're pushing a frequency band toward the **front** of your mix.

With **Transient Reduction** you're pushing it **back** with relation to everything else.

With **Volume Leveling** you're actually holding a frequency band in place so it doesn't move toward the **front** or **back** of your mix. This is effective when you've already EQ'd your instrument and have it tonally sitting where you want. But as you're aware, once you've EQ'd something it won't necessarily stay where you've placed it because the sound itself can have dynamically changing frequencies. This could be for a multitude of reasons ranging from play style to filter automation.

This technique and the next technique (#13) are two of the best examples of how multiband compression can be used to create more **Front** to **Back** depth.

Every track has a lead and every track has supporting instruments, generally referred to as pads, chords. Supporting instruments are generally meant to sit in the background with relation to your lead.

The challenge with supporting instruments as you finalize your mix is that you've spent all this time mixing at the individual track level and everything will be 85 – 90% good enough. That last 10 or 15% is actually achieved at the group/bus/mastering stage.

17 Powerful Multiband Compression Techniques | 89

So here's what we do at the group stage in order to create more Front/Back separation.

All we need to do is multiband compress whichever frequency ranges of our supporting instruments get most in the way of our leads.

This is best achieved by using a gentle and wide frequency band at 800hz – 5khz on the supporting instrument group. Here's how:

1. Set the Frequency Band to 800hz - 5khz.
2. Set Attack 10ms.
3. Set Release 30ms.
4. Set Ratio 2:1.
5. Bring your threshold down until you get .5 – 2db of gain reduction.

You're not applying any makeup gain because you're just trying to get this frequency range a little more pushed back without affecting the rest of the frequencies of your supporting instruments. It's a very transparent way of achieving greater **Front** to **Back** depth.

The reason it's transparent is because it's only happening across one section of the frequency range. The 2nd reason is because this gain reduction won't always be happening, simply because all your supporting instruments won't always play at the same exact volume.

Using multiband compression like this affords you some last minute mix separation between the instruments before you glue them together at the master. Most importantly, this way of mixing is stress-free.

It's stress-free because you don't have to go back to each instrument and figure out how to EQ them individually. You already finished that stage because at some point you have to keep moving forward or you won't finish.

Finishes are monumentally more important than perfect mixes. Subjectively 'Perfect' mixes only happen after you've mastered the art of finishing things when you decide to get them done.

At the group level if I multiband compress, I always place the multiband compressor before the bus compressor. That is simply because a multiband compressor is just an EQ on steroids and I most always EQ before bus compression.

#12
Multiband Compressing Reverb for Increased Front/Back Depth

This is hands down one of the coolest and easiest ways to gently control and shape reverb in your mix. It's primarily aimed at those of us in electronic music, but it can be used in any genre.

This technique is about sending all your reverb sends in a mix to the same group and then on that group you have a multiband compressor. **(If you've already read the 3-Space Reverb Framework, this does not include your Master Reverb, that one goes straight to the master. If you want to shape the Master Reverb, then you simply EQ it directly.)**

The multiband compressor on this group will be configured to bring down the volume of a specific frequency range of all the reverbs together whenever it gets densely populated by many instruments.

This typically happens during choruses or any time you have a synth feeding heavily into the reverb and the synth undergoes filter automation which gradually lets more and more frequency content in.

So you'll be setting up the multiband compressor so that it only reduces the volume of a given frequency band of all the reverbs during only those parts of your track where it's gotten very dense.

Even though it's not typically a good idea to compress reverb, since we are using it on a specific band, and doing it very gently the effect won't be noticeable.

This effect and the way I'm showing it to you actually creates more **front** to **back** separation in your mix by gently and transparently pushing the entirety of the reverb space of your mix back. As a result all your instrumentation will actually play slightly more forward and so this creates more depth. This is very useful for those of us that are addicted to drenching things in reverb.

Here's how:

1. Route all your Reverbs to the same group/bus.
2. Add Multiband Compressor to the Reverb group.
3. Set the Frequency Band 1khz – 5khz (this is the main area for leads and important stuff in your mix).
4. Set Attack 30ms.
5. Set Release 60 – 100ms.
6. Set Ratio 2:1.

17 Powerful Multiband Compression Techniques | 93

7. While the entire track is playing during a busy part (i.e. chorus) bring the Threshold down until you get .5 - 2db of gain reduction.

Most of the time I aim for about 1db of gain reduction and this works well.

It's particularly transparent because the treatment is happening on such a narrow band, but at the same time there are other instruments in front of the reverb which are taking your attention away from the treatment effect. So any potential side-effect is being hidden by important stuff.

Again the goal is to make it so that if you have a really dense part of your mix where reverb energy gets a bit overwhelming then this technique will fix that.

#13
Sidechain Multiband Compression for Increased Kick Punch

This technique is one of my favorite things to do as a finishing touch in my tracks right before mastering. It's a really simple way of cleaning and calibrating the low end of your mix so that it gets more power while creating more space for your kick to literally punch through your mix.

If you're familiar with sidechain compression of your bass to your kick then this will make sense to you.

This technique is meant to work alongside basic kick-bass sidechain compression, but it allows you to do a little more fine tuning of this relationship while gently and transparently opening up some space in the 0 - 150hz range of your bass so your kick can really come through.

This won't always be necessary, but once try it you'll probably become addicted to it. It's like Febreezing™ your low end in a finished track. Everything is already clean, you don't need it, but it just feels so right.

This technique works when you have all your bass instrumentation coming into a group where you can put a multiband compressor on it. This multiband compressor will allow you selectively duck just the 0hz – 150hz frequencies of our bass which will open up room for your kick. Here's how:

1. Set Low Frequency Band from 0hz – 150hz.
2. Set Attack 0ms.
3. Set Release 40ms.
4. Set Ratio 2:1.
5. As your entire mix is playing, bring down the threshold of your compressor until you feel you've opened just enough space for you kick to punch through more cleanly.

Don't overdo this technique. You worked hard at the individual track mixing stage and so you should only need anywhere from .5 – 2db of gain reduction in most cases.

If you really want to hear the benefit then add an EQ at the end of your master and apply a low pass filter and bring it all the way down to about 100hz - 150hz so that you only hear the low frequencies.

This will help you to focus on just the low frequencies and really hear what's going on in your mixes.

I call that my Low Frequency Microscope trick—it's awesome. I use it all the time when mixing. I always have a bypassed EQ on my master with this already setup and I can enable and disable it any time I want to focus on my low-end engineering.

#14
Sidechain Multiband Compression for Improved Lead Clarity

This is a variation of the technique above only now we are using it for leads.

You may already be aware of the technique of sidechain compressing a delay with the instrument that's feeding the delay. It's increasingly common that newer delay plugins include this ducking feature. That's what we're doing here, only now we're going to be ducking a supporting instrument with relation to our lead instrument.

Depending on the style of music you're working in you can get away with increasingly dramatic and creative levels of this effect. Keep in mind that this works best on instruments which play intermittently. So sustain sounds won't work so well. Here's how:

1. Add a Multiband Compressor to the supporting instrument group.
2. Set a Frequency Band on the supporting instrument group. The range of the frequency band will be across the main frequency region of your lead (usually anywhere from 1 – 8khz).

3. Route the lead to the Sidechain of the multiband compressor.
4. Set Attack 10ms.
5. Set Release 30 - 60ms.
6. Set Ratio 2:1.
7. As everything plays, bring your Threshold down until you get some gain reduction and a pleasant kind of ducking of just that frequency range in the supporting instruments.

We use a fast attack so it sucks any transient energy and forwardness out of the pads the moment the lead hits.

Release settings are up to you, but generally you want the release somewhere in the 30 - 60ms range so the volume of the support instrumentation transparently returns back to normal when your lead stops playing.

There are subtle ways and not so subtle ways of doing this. This is actually a surprisingly effective way at keeping chord/piano/supporting instruments full sounding whenever they are playing by themselves, but whenever the lead instrument plays, the problematic frequency range gets reduced which gives more space for your lead to soar.

#15
Vocal De-Essing

The goal of any De-Essing is to remove undesirable sibilance you hear in a sound. Typical usage is whenever a vocalist does an 'S' sound as it usually creates a very unpleasant spike in the frequencies in the 5khz range.

There are dedicated de-essers for this, but I don't always find them to be as transparent as using a multiband compressor. That being said I am lazy, so most of the time I'm reaching for my De-Esser since it's a simple one-stop shop.

If I'm using multiband compression to De-Ess it's because:

1. I need to really see what I'm doing.
2. I need more surgical control of the sibilance.

Here's how you Vocal De-Ess:

1. Setup a frequency band from 3khz - 7khz. Everyone's a bit different so you'll have to sweep the band in solo to find the epicenter of a person's sibilance.
2. Set Attack 10ms.
3. Set Release 15ms.

4. Set Ratio 2:1.
5. Bring Threshold down until compression is only being triggered by the sibilance of the performer. It's ok if it triggers slightly on other sounds too. You just want it triggering more on the 'S' because that's where you've set it up.

The frequency range you set to catch a person's sibilance will be different on a per individual basis. However, the epicenter of everyone's sibilance is between 3khz – 7khz. It could taper off into the 10khz, especially with certain mics, so feel free to set your own band.

I personally use these same exact settings on myself but to reduce nasality in my recordings.

I do it by way of a spectrum analyzer and me nasally going "**NNnnn**owwwww"" into a mic. This way I'm able to find the nasality and annihilate it.

This brings up the question, "Nathan do you multiband compress vocals? " And my answer is yes, yes I do. I have no idea why I find it so nice, but I do. I feel like there's a special place in mixing hell for me for doing this, but I have an ear and it has desires and I'm its slave.

600hz - 4khz is the range where nasality happens. Most people have at least two distinct resonances in this range and so for that technique I use two frequency bands. We'll explain it next as it's essential to creating broadcast vocals.

#16
Broadcast Vocals

Broadcast vocals are the perfectly smooth voices you hear on the radio, with deep low ends, and a pleasant mid range and a gently rolled off top end.

Why am I showing you this in a book primarily geared toward music? Because everyone deserves to have the confidence boosting experience of hearing what their voice sounds like when it's turned into pure sex.

So here's how we do it.

There will be 3 frequency bands:

Bass Band: From 0-150hz.

Midrange Band: From 600hz – 5khz.

Presence and Clarity Band: From 8khz – 20khz.

These are ballpark figures here, but notice that I skip 150hz – 600hz. I generally don't treat this range because it doesn't need it. 150hz – 600hz has generally always sounded weird to me when its compressed for vocals. I don't know why, it just does.

So let's start with the Bass Band.

Bass Band:

1. Set Frequency Range from 0hz – 150hz.
2. Set Attack 25ms.
3. Set Release 30ms.
4. Set Ratio 2:1.
5. Start adding 1 – 5db of Makeup Gain.
6. Bring down the Threshold to catch any of the already loud portions of your vocals bass frequencies.

The more gain reduction you achieve along with equal amounts of makeup gain, the more consistent and powerful your bass will appear. This is the literal definition of volume leveling, since coupling each db of makeup gain with a corresponding db of gain reduction means you're progressively bringing the loud parts of the signal closer in volume to the quiet parts of the signal.

Midrange Band:

1. Set Frequency Range 800hz – 5khz.
2. Set Attack 15ms.
3. Set Release 30ms.
4. Set Ratio 2:1.
5. While listening to the voice, bring down the threshold until it sounds smoother and less in your face nasally. For my voice I sometimes get

about 5db of gain reduction, so it's substantial for me.

Bringing this frequency range down is what allows a voice to play louder without being overwhelming. In the context of dense mixes, it's a little counter-intuitive because we tend to let this play a little more intensely than we would by itself as it allows the voice to dominate in denser mixes.

As an example, when I'm singing in songs I don't always compress this range. I also sing differently than I speak and I would personally consider myself as having the same singing prowess as a goat. But like many artists, I'm brutally self-critical.

Presence and Clarity Band:

1. From 5khz – 20khz.
2. Set Attack 15ms.
3. Set Release 20ms.
4. Set Ratio 2:1.
5. Bring Threshold down until you get .5 - 2db of gain reduction

For this band I typically don't use any makeup gain as the majority of mics hype this frequency range anyway.

What we're actually doing here is what I call pseudo-sibilance control. While sibilance is mainly centered in the 5khz range, some of it tapers all the way up to the 20khz range. So we compress this range to catch any sibilance that remains.

Getting smooth broadcast vocals is a very subjective thing, but the general shaping that's happening is a boosting of the <150hz frequencies, a reducing in the 800hz – 5khz frequency ranges to allow for more volume without harshness and a compression of 8khz + to soften the pseudo-sibilance that's happening.

None of these bands are dedicated toward directly handling sibilance. You should use a dedicated de-esser or another multiband compressor before your broadcast multiband compressor to selectively compress the sibilance range as I showed you in the De-Essing Technique earlier.

We De-Ess before any compression (multiband or single-band) because I'd rather not have sibilance acting to trigger my compressor in any way. It also follows the rule of doing cutting based EQ decisions before compressing.

De-Essing is very much a form of cutting EQ and since it's cutting away sibilance it makes sense to follow it with compression because that's what sounds more natural.

Whether to use EQ before compression is a topic that's hotly and perhaps even erotically debated amongst keyboard warrior/audio engineers who spend more time talking about the **'right way'** to make music than actually making it.

I don't really care much for that debate because I know that really good composers have a skilled ear for sound and this good ear can massively compensate for limited mixing skills, not knowing how to tie their shoelaces, or what the phase difference between linear-phase and minimum-phase processing is.

The only thing I remember is linear phase sounds better. Only use it on the master or your computer will throw itself off a bridge. On the way down it will commit Sepuku, aka Samurai Suicide and discover the theory of everything, but it won't get to share it—all because you linear phased on things that weren't your master. What a sad day for humanity.

#17
Mastering Multiband Compression

I've always felt that 50% of mastering is peak control. I should probably write another book on just controlling peaks, called Peaking, "How a mastering engineer finally peaked by conquering his greatest peak, peak volume."

The 1st line would be something like:

"It was the Mount Everest of audio peaks. Littered along the path we're SSL's, 1176s, La2as and an abnormal amount of Waves L1's."

When I say peaks I mean if you have a bunch of instruments and they play comfortably together at -10db, and then your kick comes to party and your master volume jump up to -2dbs, then my friend you've got a major peakage problem.

Of course kicks and snares are the main offenders of peak control, learning to keep them controlled without sucking the life out of them is an art in and of itself.

My second book about peak control will be a romance novella called "Peaking 2: I thought I peaked, but then I unmated my kick and snare."

I love that word, peaking, everywhere, everywhere except when mixing. God I hate peaks when mixing.

Anyway, so in a perfect utopia you wouldn't have to do any peak control at the master channel, but that's generally not the case.

We're controlling peaks because we want all our instrumentation to hit our limiter at about the same time. Most of the time your kick and snare will be hitting the limiter anywhere from 2 - 5 dB to months before anything else.

The greater the distance between the peaks of your kick/snare and everything else in your mix, the more difficult it becomes to cleanly "louden up" your mix.

I told myself I wasn't going to write a book on Mastering, even though we're talking about multiband compression, the belligerent, alcoholic father of the mastering engineer in therapy.

Mastering and multiband compression practically go hand in hand, this is something I don't totally agree with as you can easily destroy a well put together mix with multiband compression on the master.

17 Powerful Multiband Compression Techniques | 109

For this reason I'm showing you a surgical and goal oriented way of using multiband compression on the master--namely peak control.

Now when it comes to mastering you have 4 main frequency ranges where you might want a bit of peak control. These 4 frequency ranges are basically described in my 4-Zone Mix Theory. They are slightly different here because these ranges tend to sound more natural on a mastering multiband compressor, but you will notice they are basically the same as what I presented you in the 4-Zone Mix Theory. So here they are:

1. **Bass:** 0hz – 150hz
2. **Body:** 150hz – 800khz
3. **Presence:** 800khz – 7khz
4. **Detail and Sizzle:** 7khz - 20khz

0 – 150hz: the bass of your mix.

Your main issue is going to be your bass layering with your kick. When these two instruments hit together you get a peak in volume. The goal is to control this peak just a little bit so the final limiter has a little easier of a time maximizing the volume of your mix. Here's how:

1. Set Frequency Band 0 – 150hz.
2. Set Attack 25ms.
3. Set Release 30ms.
4. Set Ratio 2:1.
5. Bring Threshold down until you have 1 – 3db of gain reduction

Makeup gain is an option here, but most producers suffer from the issue of too much bass when mastering time comes along. This is because of weird listening environments coupled with the joy of producing with extra bass because it's fun.

Compression of this frequency range is mainly going to be triggered by your kick. When the bass plays by itself it generally won't trigger compression.

Overly compressing bass mostly sounds horrible. For those of you that are very precise with your individual kick and bass mixing you may not even need to touch this band.

Like I said, I use this to reduce peak volume of my bass, not to add volume to my bass. That's generally not needed for most producers.

150hz – 800hz: the body of your mix.

17 Powerful Multiband Compression Techniques | 111

It's the one range I don't like touching with a multiband compressor.

My experiences have told me this is the one range you really need to get right with individual and group based mixing.

I would much rather rely on gentle EQing in this range. Multiband compressing in it doesn't sound good to me. But if you have peaks or issues with levels then you can use the peak control and leveling techniques I've already showed you with surprisingly clean results.

If you feel the need to reduce peaks in this range here's how I would do it, even though it feels like walking on a minefield with industrial magnets attached to my legs:

1. Set Frequency Band 150hz – 800hz.
2. Set Attack 20ms.
3. Set Release 20ms.
4. Set Ratio 2:1.
5. Bring threshold down until any peaks get reduced to a level you like.

You shouldn't need to add makeup gain if you're just trying to control peaks. If you're trying to volume level dynamic frequencies in this range then you'll probably like adding about as much make-up gain as you achieve from gain reduction.

800hz – 7khz: the presence and intelligibility of your mix.

The major problems in this range have to do with the fact that this is the major sensitive range of human hearing.

For most producers it isn't actually that they've improperly mixed this range, it's that the louder we boost a mix with a limiter, the more this range sticks out, despite the fact that everything else got boosted.

This has to do with the fact that human hearing is non-linear with relation to increasing loudness. This means that what sounds balanced and fine at -15db in this range, can often sound overwhelming at 0db.

This has to do with the Fletcher-Munson curve, and if you look it up you'll eventually realize that Mastering is the process of in many ways, creating the inverse of that curve.

As a simple example since our hearing is really sensitive at 2khz, we tend to actually EQ cut in this range when mastering so the mix can be played louder without making us want to claw our ears off.

So after the typical wide and gentle EQ cut that very often happens between 800hz – 5khz, the typically most offending peak instruments in this range are transients from your kick, snares, and crazy lead instrument stuff.

So the goal is to catch just those peaks, **without always** compressing this range. This should be easy since peaks will throw the volume past your threshold and thus trigger compression. And when the peaks go away on their own, your triggering volume should fall enough that gain reduction goes away or decreases noticeably.

Here's how to configure it:

1. Set Frequency Range 800hz – 5khz
2. Set Attack 15ms.
3. Set Release 15ms.
4. Set Ratio 2:1.
5. Bring Threshold down until the transients of your kick and snare start to trigger compression. You want about 1 - 3db of gain reduction.

Again makeup gain is a selective choice here, if you find that you need a deeper threshold to really push those transients back then you might need to apply some makeup gain.

That being said, you'd be amazed how this range is repeatedly and unceremoniously sacrificed in order to create a louder, more consistent and pleasing listening experience at all volume levels. The key phrase there is 'all volume levels."

What a lot of people don't realize about mastering is that it isn't just making your track better, but it's also making some small, necessary sacrifices to normalize your mix for a lot of different playback systems. Not everyone has that godly listening system you've been producing on. Some people listen on North Korean Laptop Speakers.

7khz – 20khz: the sizzle and sparkle of your mix.

This is also where hi-hats and cymbals come to die during mastering. Unfortunately, these guys tend to become a bit too sibilant and sizzly the more you attempt to increase volume via limiting.

One of the ways we can hide this with multiband compression is to kill a little bit of their transient information.

This is somewhere between volume leveling and transient control. In effect we are aiming to tame the transients and volume levels of our 10khz+ frequencies with relation to the other multiband decisions we just made.

For this reason I always multiband compress this frequency last.

Here's how to control them:

1. Set Frequency Range 7khz - 20khz.
2. Set Attack 5 - 10ms.
3. Set Release 5 - 10ms.
4. Set Ratio 2:1.
5. Bring Threshold down until you get .5 - 2db of gain reduction.

Again makeup gain is dependent upon how much you want to diminish the transient energy and hype-ness of this range.

The more you need to diminish the transient energy in this range, the more you may need to add up to half your gain reduction. So if you get 3db of gain reduction, then 1.5db of makeup gain.

That being said I like there to be dynamics in this range, otherwise it gets very fatiguing. It's for this reason that I prefer to control transient peaks in this range with multiband compression and then avoid make-up gain. It sounds more natural.

Just remember, that our ears find leveling and overall average volume increases in this range very tiring.

That's why in this range I tend to aim for .5 - 3db of gain reduction being triggered off my hats, cymbals and snares, and maybe noise sweeps and that's it.

If I have some serious peakage from the cymbals it would be much better to go handle them at the individual track or drum group where you could get away with more aggressive mix decisions.

In fact sometimes I find myself using this exact technique directly on the drum group because like I said, I can get away with a bit more involved treatment there. This would hide the treatment more effectively as long as the main issue was just elements in your drum group.

When in doubt do the mixing at the individual track level. When in doubt **AND lazy** do the treatment at the group/bus level.

Zen and the Art of Multiband Compression

Multiband compression causes everyone stress at some point, except for the people who avoid it all together.

I hated stressing about it and because of that I've tried my best to concisely give you the techniques I use. I hope you'll understand that there's really just two ways you can use a multiband compressor:

1. **Transient Control**
    a. Transient Enhancement
    b. Transient Reduction
2. **Volume Leveling**

Once you realize that you're just using multiband compression to make volume more consistent or to just control transients on a per-frequency-band-basis then it makes it a lot simpler to achieve blend/contrast.

It's not as difficult of a tool as it's made out to be, but only as long as you know whether you're trying to achieve volume leveling or transient control with it and whether you're trying to achieve those for more blend or contrast.

I can assure you that no one 'really' knows the exact or right way to use a multiband compressor because in the end it's a shaping tool. And since every sculptor uses a chisel a bit differently, you have every right to find your own way.

My hope is that by understanding the two main ways we use multiband compression: for **Volume Leveling** and **Transient Control**, that you can quickly decide how to use it in your future projects.

I also hope that you understand the value of just using 1 or 2 bands. You shouldn't be using all 4 on a regular basis.

For me personally, 80% of the time its 1 or 2 bands. The other 15% it's 3 bands and last 5% it's all 4 bands—typically in mastering situations. In mastering I very often use just 3 bands, because as I've said I don't like compressing the entirety of my 150hz - 800hz range. I honestly feel that should be handled with individual track and group mixing.

Remember that while single-band compression does shape sounds, it's limited in its ability to dynamically shape the frequency content of a sound the way a multiband compressor can.

It is my sincere hope that this book continues helping you master multiband compression.

Feel free to re-read it anytime you want to touch up with your multiband-compression technique. Learning is a process of repetition, and with repetition eventually anything you're unsure of will literally figure itself out just because you've done it enough times. That means you don't have to know what you're doing at first, you just need to do it.

If you don't know why or how something works, just continue messing with it a little here and a little there, because eventually your subconscious will connect the dots and you'll get that "aha!" moment.

Additional Resources

SEE FOLLOWING PAGES
FOR FREE PREVIEWS OF EACH BOOK

Books by the Author:

The EQ and Compression Formula: *Learn the step by step way to use EQ and Compression together*
https://amzn.to/2FbCubN

The 3-Space Reverb Framework: Learn the step by step system for using reverb in your mixes
https://amzn.to/2JlN4zy

The Bus Compression Framework: *The set and forget way to get an INSTANTLY professional sounding mix*
https://amzn.to/2wzixN1

Nathan's Top 20 Plugins

Includes 3 of my most **Massive Engineering Secrets** that I won't **REVEAL** anywhere else!

[See Page-131 for the Top 20 Plugins]

Free Music Production/Audio Engineering Resources
http://www.mybeatlab.com/tutorials

Book Previews

The EQ and Compression Formula: Learn the step by step way to use EQ and Compression Together

Visit: https://amzn.to/2FbCubN

The Rule of 300

One of the most frustrating issues many producers encounter is a muddy or undefined low end in their mixes. Producers run into this problem because the instruments occupying the 20hz to 400hz frequency range of their mix are having a conflict catastrophe.

The reality is 20hz – 400hz is the most difficult frequency range for us to master because our hearing isn't as adapted to noticing details in it.

In order to avoid this temporary, but inherent weakness in our low end hearing there is one simple rule we can follow—The Rule of 300.

The rule of 300 states that if it isn't bass, kick or snare, then you must high pass those instruments at 300hz or higher.

The higher you can get away with the better for your mix.

This rule eliminates the main causes of a muddy mix because as you now know we run into this problem when our 20hz to 400hz range is swamped by too many competing instruments.

When professional mixers talk about balance they mean it as if there's a balance scale in front of you and so imagine on the one end there is something heavy, and the other has something light. And like a balance scale **you must be very selective about which instrument(s) are frequency 'heavy' and which ones are frequency 'light.'**

Balance just means that it sounds pleasing to you, but when mixers talk about balance they mean that you're decisive about which instruments get to be frequency dense and which one's get to be frequency light in a given frequency zone.

By following this rule your mixes will immediately start occupying the top 5% of mixes out there.

The 3-Space Reverb Framework: Learn the step by step system for using reverb in your mixes

Visit: https://amzn.to/2JlN4zy

The Mastering Reverb

Adding the same reverb to everything in your mix is the ultimate glue technique. If you aren't already then once you start doing this your mixes will hit a new level that you simply couldn't imagine.

Pros will occasionally mention they do this, but they often don't talk about how substantially it brings everything together in your mix. Put simply, it's better than bus compression at gluing things together, and bus compression is literally referred to as 'the glue.'

The trick with using reverb on your master is to create what I call a premaster reverb track and to then route every instrument/fx/send (everything) through this track. The premaster reverb track is then routed directly to your master. You will then create a separate Master Reverb Send where your master reverb goes. This master reverb send is routed directly to your master.

You will then use the premaster reverb track to send a small portion of the its volume to your master reverb. The Master Reverb should be using a small room preset with .3 - .7sec of decay. You'll want to low-cut frequencies (<200hz) on your master reverb because you just won't need those, otherwise they will swamp your mix.

From the premaster track you can control how much all the instruments in your track are feeding this final reverb. The idea is to feed the master verb somewhat lightly so that it's almost imperceptible, but you can get fairly aggressive with this and that is very enjoyable to do as well.

This final reverb is meant to emulate the room your track is playing in. Like if you were playing your track through speakers in a club, this is what the master reverb is emulating, albeit with a much shorter decay. I don't know why, but it really makes a song come together in the most simply, impressive way.

This master reverb treatment happens pre-master, hence the pre-master reverb track we used. This does mean that I like running the Master Reverb +

everything else in my session through my entire master treatment chain. There's nothing wrong with this for me because I don't rely too much on extreme forms of mastering for my projects.

That being said, one of the symptoms of heavy loudness maximization on your master is that the stereo width/intelligibility of your track tends to go down. This can be remedied by configuring a master reverb on your project right before your final limiter.

This is just me getting into mix-engineer porn at this point, but the idea would be doing your entire master chain, except for your final limiter on a **'pre-master treatment track.'** You then send a little bit of your 'premaster treatment track' signal to your master reverb send, and then mix these all together at your Master right before the limiter.

This allows our master reverb to be unaffected by your mastering chain. What's really cool is that the heavy-handed effects of your pre-master treatment will influence the sounds going into your master reverb and all this is happening without the master chain negatively impacting your master reverb's stereo information and acoustics.

This is powerful because reverb information suffers the most from heavy compression and limiting. It's also an advanced technique that underlines the best mastering technique, namely that all really good mastering is a means of hiding the side-effects of mastering.

It works to hide mastering because while everything was heavily processed in your pre-mastering chain you're restoring some naturalness to it by running it through a reverb after the fact. And that reverb is only running into a limiter before your track is mixed down. It's this sequence that acts to hide mastering artifacts like multiband compression/limiter pumping.

***The Bus Compression Framework**: The set and forget way to get an INSTANTLY professional sounding mix*

Visit: https://amzn.to/2wzixN1

Why Do We Call It Pocket Compression? (Instead of Bus Compression)

The reason I call this pocket compression is because the compressor action creates an artificial pocket around instruments within a compression group. This artificial pocket has the characteristic of giving all those instruments similar dynamic behavior.

When I say dynamic similarity I mean that the volume of all the instruments in that group is changing in relation to our bus compressor being triggered.

Because any instrument or simultaneous playing of instruments within a group could trigger compressor action, it means that every instrument plays a part in the group's dynamic behavior which is the point of bus compression.

When I say "compressor behavior" I mean the increasing/decreasing of gain reduction. The rate and speed at which gain reduction increases/diminishes is the result of your attack and release settings.

It should be noted that within a bus compression group there's typically a few louder instruments that have a greater impact on the behavior of the compressor.

Other instruments are often too quiet to actually trigger or have a big influence on the compressors behavior. A good example of this would be in a drum bus.

In a drum bus the compressor movement is typically being driven by your kick and snare. Hi-hats don't generally trigger the compressor and this is because they usually aren't loud enough to do so.

Now with bus compression you're actually using a compressor to give instruments specific time-dependent volume characteristics. That's just a fancy way of saying you're making instruments within a group breathe relative to one another. As I've mentioned with my technique, this breathing/pumping is so subtle that it actually glues instruments together dynamically.

The dynamic glue we're talking about is this subtle rhythmic pumping/breathing. The rate and speed of the subtle pumping/breathing is the result of your attack and release settings.

The other glue effect we've already mentioned is simply the fact that all bus compressors impart a subtle and transparent form of saturation across all instruments running through them. This saturation simply adds harmonics to these instruments in about the same way in about the same place. This subtly unifies the "tone signature" of all our instruments which gives our mixes a professional sense of cohesion.

Now with my technique I simply use SSL bus compressors. They're perfect and there's a reason everyone loves them. This imparts the same saturation across all instruments no matter what group they're being sent to, thus gluing and unifying the tone of my entire mix.

Now with pocket compression we are deliberately forcing instruments to behave the same in relation to the compressor they're going into.

My favorite way to think about it is imagine you've got an elastic balloon around a group of instruments. The compressor settings determine how much space there is between the balloon edges and the instruments. This amount of space is the same thing as your Threshold setting.

At some point your instruments will get so loud that they fill in this extra space and begin to press against the edges of your balloon. How stretchy or not stretchy the balloon is is determined by your Ratio.

A 2:1 Ratio is the best stretchiness for this balloon, virtually always.

The rate and speed at which the balloon stretches when instruments get too loud and press into its edges is determined by your Attack and Release settings.

And so with bus compression you're limiting the volume freedom of instruments as if there was an elastic balloon being placed around them preventing them from moving too far beyond the initial boundaries of the balloon.

It's this artificial effect of creating an elastic boundary around instruments that is pocket compression.

This main idea is so simple, and amazingly powerful because it means that faster attacks (.1 - 3ms) and slower releases (.6 - 1sec) pushes stuff in the back of the mix, which creates **blend** and slower attacks (10 - 30ms) and fast releases (.1 - .3sec) allow grouped instruments to remain more open, dynamic and in front of the mix which creates **contrast**.

Nathan's Top 20 Plugins

As a gift for reading this far I'm going to be revealing 3 of my biggest engineering secrets and the exact plugins I use to achieve them. This is the only place you'll ever find this stuff so give it a read and prepare to upgrade your mixes!

Aside from Verbsuite Classics I've consistently used each processor within this list for 3 – 8 years. I strongly believe in these tools.

I will only use plugins that sound great and which are efficient and easy to use. Simplicity and speed is crucial for consistently getting into a creative flow and so I only use tools which support that.

I already went through the 6 years of trying/owning 500+ plugins and trying out that many plugins was a big waste of time and only hindered my improvement.

It is my sincere hope that this list will save you the time I lost, because today I only have 40 or so plugins and these are the Top 20 I couldn't live without.

Digital EQ (Transparent EQ)

FabFilter Pro-Q 2

This is my workhorse EQ. I use it about 90% of the time. The other 10% is character EQing. It has an excellent graphical interface and is by far the easiest EQ to use. It's extremely transparent which means you won't hear it negatively affecting the sound. It contains essential mid/side processing as well as linear phase settings for use in mastering.

Visit: http://bit.ly/2Ip04rh

Analog EQ's (Character EQ's)

Virtual Mix Rack 2.0

Contains two Analog EQ's: FG-N and FG-S as well as an amazing compressor (FG-401) and 1176 Limiter. I classify these as "Character EQ's." I only use these EQ's for boosting because of their lush and vibrant boost-dependent saturation. Whereas a regular digital EQ like FabFilter Pro-Q 2 is going to transparently shape a sound, these EQ's will literally breathe life into dull and lifeless sources. You only need to hear the boosts to become a believer.

Visit: http://bit.ly/2jMqky7

Bus Compressors

Virtual Bus Compressors

Virtual Bus Compressors contains 3 of the most popular bus compressors emulations including an SSL Bus compressor (FG-Grey). Using these on a mix in the multi-layered way I teach in **The Bus Compression Framework** will kill any of the blandness inherent in digital recordings. The FG-Grey alone is worth the price tag, but you get 2 bonus legendary bus compressors. I really couldn't live without the FG-Grey because its saturation characteristics are 60 - 70% responsible for the professional signature of my sound.

Visit: http://bit.ly/2wvVHGk

Compressors

FabFilter Pro-C 2

This is the Swiss Army knife of compressors. It can do any kind of sound from smooth and transparent all the way to snappy and aggressive pumping. I use it for everything, especially if I'm unsure what compressor to use. With its easy to understand visual display it's the most noob friendly and educational compressor there is. If I had started with this compressor I probably would of learned how to use compression about 50% faster. It has deep sidechaining capabilities as well as multiple compressor styles making it's the best all around compressor. If I could only live with one compressor this would be it.

Visit: http://bit.ly/2FZfYnb

FG-401 (Part of Virtual Mix Rack 2.0)
My go to vocal compressor/LA-2A on steroids. It's capable of being extremely transparent and gentle on sounds while bathing them in a heavenly layer of saturation. You have the option of enabling/disabling the saturation stage of this compressor which is awesome. I use this as a transparent volume leveler/tone enrichment tool. I don't use it for enhancing transients or the body of sounds as I personally feel it's too gentle for this. I primarily use the FG 401 as more flexible and configurable LA-2A.

Visit: http://bit.ly/2jMqky7

De-Essers

FabFilter Pro-DS
For me personally I find this to be the easiest and most versatile De-Esser there is. I used the Waves De-Esser before this, but this one is significantly better sounding and more flexible. If you record vocals and you're sick of sibilance this is the cure.

Visit: http://bit.ly/2rv904W

Limiter

FabFilter Pro-L 2
This is my all around workhorse limiter/mastering limiter. It's very easy to use and sounds absolutely amazing. I use it for mastering as well as individual track limiting/clipping. It's incredibly flexible with multiple limiting algorithms, oversampling as well as adjustable attack and release settings. I've used a lot of different limiters over many years--this is the one that stayed and for good reason.

Visit: http://bit.ly/2ws1pJn

Multiband Compressors

FabFilter Pro-MB

This is my go to multiband compressor because it's the easiest to use. It's exquisitely transparent and musical sounding. I've used a lot of multiband compressors over the years—this one is King. With per-band sidechains, upwards and downwards compression/expansion it's the most flexible, easy to use multiband dynamic processor there is. As with all FabFilter plugins the visual interface is a cut above the rest.

Visit: http://bit.ly/2KK3Xp3

Multiband Distortion

Kombinat TRI

Too many multiband distortion processors are bloated with a confusing amount of features. I love the ease and simplicity of this one. I pretty much only use the Saturation, Clipping, Fuzz, and Tube Clip distortion algorithms with Saturation getting the heaviest use.

Visit: http://bit.ly/2FZvr6o

FXpansion Maul

This is actually the best and simultaneously most analog sounding multiband distortion out there. It's a little deeper than Kombinat TRI, but it's still the 2nd simplest multiband distortion out there. As far as I'm concerned FXpansion nailed the sound of this with their proprietary DCAM-modeled diode, tube and transistor based circuits along with clippers, overdrives and waveshapers. This thing is an absolute beast.

Visit: http://bit.ly/2jMjpoC

Modulation

Soundtoys PhaseMistress

I've tried more phasers than I can count and Phasemistress is the best. It can do every phasing sound you dream of. You really won't need to tweak it outside of frequency, depth and rate because of its more than 60+ phaser styles that you can select on the fly. If you're a tweaker then it also gives you access to much deeper controls as well.

Visit: http://bit.ly/2wBlRYn

Valhalla UberMod

This is categorically the best chorusing effect out there. It can do everything from chorusing to flanging as well as delays. It's an incredibly flexible and easy to use tool. Once upon a time I owned an Eventide H3000 and I look at this plugin as its twin brother.

Visit: http://bit.ly/2jMw1vZ

Xfer LFO Tool

Tremolo allows us to rhythmically shape the volume of a sound. Conventionally, tremolo is used for kick based sidechain compression. But LFO tool allows you to achieve much more exotic results. It allows for rhythmic control of volume, panning, and a variety of filters. Once you begin looking at tremolo as way to create rhythmic texture and movement within your projects it will completely change how you design and engineer your music.

Visit: http://bit.ly/2Iso2SE

Saturation

Soundtoys Radiator
I almost retired this plugin until I discovered its power on vocals. It can take a $100 mic recording and turn it into a $1000 dollar mic recording. I don't typically drive it very hard, but adding it to vocals and lightly turning up the hi-frequency gain instantly makes vocals cut through a mix like a hot knife through butter.

Visit: http://bit.ly/2G2g3pY

Virtual Console Collection 2.0
This plugin emulates the extremely musical and transparent saturation of analog consoles. Another secret you'd only find here: 50% of Nathan's super awesome sound is that he uses VCC feeding into FG-Grey on each of the 5 buses/groups described in **The Bus Compression Framework** (I use the same console emulation for all 5 groups but I don't use VCC on the master). So

Secret: All 5 buses: VCC > FG-Grey

Visit: http://bit.ly/2G0L5P5

Tape Simulation

Slate Digital Virtual Tape Machines

This is my favorite tape machine for saturating leads and anything that doesn't have sub (<100hz) energy in it. It's one of the best sounding tape emulations there is—I just wouldn't let it touch my basses because it pumps up the sub volume, for me, in an undesirable way. Nonetheless I use this as a warming and rounding tool for instruments that are too bright or sound to sterile. I literally just slap it on and sterility and brightness are cured.

Visit: http://bit.ly/2K82kAr

Transient Shaper

Oxford Transmod

This is the transient shaper to rule all transient shapers. It allows you to control the exact length and intensity of transient information within a signal. Something a lot of people don't think to do with these tools is to use them on leads, hi hats and other instruments where more/less attack is desired. This gives you a level of control over transient snap that no compressor can approach. Oxford Transmod is the only transient shaper

I know of that can effectively shape transients on instruments other than drums.

Visit: **http://bit.ly/2wupq2c**

Reverbs

Valhalla Room

This is my workhorse reverb. It's so flexible and easy to use that you can never go wrong with using it. In my opinion it's the best reverb for ambient styles as well as aggressive styles as the decay length can be set as long as you need. I'm a huge fan of this developer.

Visit: **http://bit.ly/2KacFfp**

Verbsuite Classics

Here's another Easter egg for you. In *The 3-Space Reverb Framework* I talk about how to use a Master reverb to glue your mix together. I also mentioned that your master reverb should be different from your other reverbs. This is my master reverb. It's perfect for anything with a shorter decay (<2sec). I don't feel it's strong for long-decay reverb like Valhalla Room. But the clarity, depth and space this reverb creates is 2nd to none which is why it's my Master reverb.

Visit: **http://bit.ly/2wauPLU**

Softube TSAR-1 Reverb

In my opinion this is the best reverb for drums. Its somewhat grainy texture makes it excellent for organic sources like Drums, Vocals and Keys. In ***The 3-Space Reverb Framework*** I talk about increasing depth by blending and contrasting different types of reverb units. As an example, whereas Valhalla Room is smooth and excels at blending, TSAR-1's grainy character is great for creating contrast and pushing instruments toward the front of your mix. I would avoid drenching an entire mix with TSAR-1 because it will devour your mixing real-estate fast. Just use it on 1, maybe two instruments or just drums and that should be it.

Visit: http://bit.ly/2I65U1i

Printed in Great Britain
by Amazon